Dear Reader,

    This workbook is a tool that can be used as you plan to intentionally lower your bills, save money, and take control of the money you have saved. I am not a financial expert, but I wanted to share my yearlong journey for saving money. This interactive book can be used in a variety of ways to meet your needs. A calendar for each month of the year can be used to track your daily spending. You may also enjoy the monthly reflections that will help you to remain focused on goals that you've set for yourself. A monthly budget is included for you to document where your money is going, and savings entry forms will allow you to see how well you are doing. These tools can be altered to best fit your needs as you set goals for financial freedom.

Best of luck,

Vanessa Wheeler

Savings Plan

Think about your yearly goal. What would you like to save by the end of the year? Be realistic. Think about your current situation and how much you are able to put back after you pay bills.

Weekly Goal _____

Monthly Goal _____

Yearly Goal _____

How are you going to make this happen? What do you plan to cut in order to meet your savings goal? This savings should be separate from your emergency fund addressed in the monthly budget.

_____

_____

_____

_____

_____

_____

_____

What will this goal help you to accomplish? What do you plan to do with the money you save?

_____

_____

_____

_____

_____

_____

_____

January-Monthly Budget

Item	Company Name	Date	Amount Paid
1. House/Rent			
2. Security Alarm			
3. Utilities			
4. Cable/Internet			
5. Home Phone			
6. Cell Phone			
7. Auto Payment #1			
8. Auto Payment #2			
9. Auto Insurance			
10. Home Warranty/Renters Insurance			
11. Life Insurance			
12. Student Loan #1			
13. Student Loan # 2			
14. Credit Card #1			
15. Credit Card #2			
16. Credit Card #3			
17. Credit Card #4			
18. Credit Card #5			
19. Household/Miscellaneous			
20. Gas			
21. Groceries			
22. Emergency Fund			
23. Savings			
24. Retirement Fund			
25. Entertainment			
26. Other			
27. Other			
28. Other			
29. Other			
30. Other			

Total Monthly Expenses _____

January-Monthly Savings Record Keeping

Designate a savings account specifically for depositing money for your savings goal. This money should not be combined with your emergency fund mentioned on the monthly budget. The goal is to refrain from withdrawing money from this account. However, if it is imperative that you withdraw money, record this as a debit to the account and calculate the new total.

Date	Amount (+, -)	Total

Amount Saved _____

January						
S	M	T	W	T	F	S
___ Spent $_____ on	___ Spent $_____ on	___ Spent $_____ on	___ Spent $_____ on	___ Spent $_____ on	___ Spent $_____ on	___ Spent $_____ on
___ Spent $_____ on	___ Spent $_____ on	___ Spent $_____ on	___ Spent $_____ on	___ Spent $_____ on	___ Spent $_____ on	___ Spent $_____ on
___ Spent $_____ on	___ Spent $_____ on	___ Spent $_____ on	___ Spent $_____ on	___ Spent $_____ on	___ Spent $_____ on	___ Spent $_____ on
___ Spent $_____ on	___ Spent $_____ on	___ Spent $_____ on	___ Spent $_____ on	___ Spent $_____ on	___ Spent $_____ on	___ Spent $_____ on
___ Spent $_____ on	___ Spent $_____ on	___ Spent $_____ on	___ Spent $_____ on	___ Spent $_____ on	___ Spent $_____ on	___ Spent $_____ on
___ Spent $_____ on	___ Spent $_____ on	___ Spent $_____ on	___ Spent $_____ on	___ Spent $_____ on	___ Spent $_____ on	___ Spent $_____ on

January-Monthly Reflection

Use your calendar to add up the total amount spent this month that was not a part of your budget.

Total Spent _____

Take a look at your monthly spending calendar. What are your thoughts on your monthly spending? How will this influence your choices for next month?

_____
_____
_____
_____
_____
_____
_____
_____

Use your monthly savings tracker to add up the total amount you saved this month.

Total Saved _____

Did you meet your monthly savings goal? What can be done? Go back and look at your monthly budget to make sure you have set a realistic savings goal.

_____
_____
_____
_____
_____
_____
_____
_____

Remember to celebrate success. What thing (within your budget) will you do to reward yourself for taking control of your financial future?

_____
_____
_____

February-Monthly Budget

Item	Company Name	Date	Amount Paid
1. House/Rent			
2. Security Alarm			
3. Utilities			
4. Cable/Internet			
5. Home Phone			
6. Cell Phone			
7. Auto Payment #1			
8. Auto Payment #2			
9. Auto Insurance			
10. Home Warranty/Renters Insurance			
11. Life Insurance			
12. Student Loan #1			
13. Student Loan # 2			
14. Credit Card #1			
15. Credit Card #2			
16. Credit Card #3			
17. Credit Card #4			
18. Credit Card #5			
19. Household/Miscellaneous			
20. Gas			
21. Groceries			
22. Emergency Fund			
23. Savings			
24. Retirement Fund			
25. Entertainment			
26. Other			
27. Other			
28. Other			
29. Other			
30. Other			

Total Monthly Expenses _____

February-Monthly Savings Record Keeping

Designate a savings account specifically for depositing money for your savings goal. This money should not be combined with your emergency fund mentioned on the monthly budget. The goal is to refrain from withdrawing money from this account. However, if it is imperative that you withdraw money, record this as a debit to the account and calculate the new total.

Date	Amount (+, -)	Total

Amount Saved _____

February						
S	M	T	W	T	F	S
___ Spent $_____ on	___ Spent $_____ on	___ Spent $_____ on	___ Spent $_____ on	___ Spent $_____ on	___ Spent $_____ on	___ Spent $_____ on
___ Spent $_____ on	___ Spent $_____ on	___ Spent $_____ on	___ Spent $_____ on	___ Spent $_____ on	___ Spent $_____ on	___ Spent $_____ on
___ Spent $_____ on	___ Spent $_____ on	___ Spent $_____ on	___ Spent $_____ on	___ Spent $_____ on	___ Spent $_____ on	___ Spent $_____ on
___ Spent $_____ on	___ Spent $_____ on	___ Spent $_____ on	___ Spent $_____ on	___ Spent $_____ on	___ Spent $_____ on	___ Spent $_____ on
___ Spent $_____ on	___ Spent $_____ on	___ Spent $_____ on	___ Spent $_____ on	___ Spent $_____ on	___ Spent $_____ on	___ Spent $_____ on
___ Spent $_____ on	___ Spent $_____ on	___ Spent $_____ on	___ Spent $_____ on	___ Spent $_____ on	___ Spent $_____ on	___ Spent $_____ on

February-Monthly Reflection

Use your calendar to add up the total amount spent this month that was not a part of your budget.

Total Spent _____

Take a look at your monthly spending calendar. What are your thoughts on your monthly spending? How will this influence your choices for next month?

_____
_____
_____
_____
_____
_____
_____

Use your monthly savings tracker to add up the total amount you saved this month.

Total Saved _____

Did you meet your monthly savings goal? What can be done? Go back and look at your monthly budget to make sure you have set a realistic savings goal.

_____
_____
_____
_____
_____
_____
_____

Remember to celebrate success. What thing (within your budget) will you do to reward yourself for taking control of your financial future?

_____
_____
_____

March-Monthly Budget

Item	Company Name	Date	Amount Paid
1. House/Rent			
2. Security Alarm			
3. Utilities			
4. Cable/Internet			
5. Home Phone			
6. Cell Phone			
7. Auto Payment #1			
8. Auto Payment #2			
9. Auto Insurance			
10. Home Warranty/Renters Insurance			
11. Life Insurance			
12. Student Loan #1			
13. Student Loan # 2			
14. Credit Card #1			
15. Credit Card #2			
16. Credit Card #3			
17. Credit Card #4			
18. Credit Card #5			
19. Household/Miscellaneous			
20. Gas			
21. Groceries			
22. Emergency Fund			
23. Savings			
24. Retirement Fund			
25. Entertainment			
26. Other			
27. Other			
28. Other			
29. Other			
30. Other			

Total Monthly Expenses _____

March-Monthly Savings Record Keeping

Designate a savings account specifically for depositing money for your savings goal. This money should not be combined with your emergency fund mentioned on the monthly budget. The goal is to refrain from withdrawing money from this account. However, if it is imperative that you withdraw money, record this as a debit to the account and calculate the new total.

Date	Amount (+, -)	Total

Amount Saved _____

March						
S	M	T	W	T	F	S
___ Spent $_____ on	___ Spent $_____ on	___ Spent $_____ on	___ Spent $_____ on	___ Spent $_____ on	___ Spent $_____ on	___ Spent $_____ on
___ Spent $_____ on	___ Spent $_____ on	___ Spent $_____ on	___ Spent $_____ on	___ Spent $_____ on	___ Spent $_____ on	___ Spent $_____ on
___ Spent $_____ on	___ Spent $_____ on	___ Spent $_____ on	___ Spent $_____ on	___ Spent $_____ on	___ Spent $_____ on	___ Spent $_____ on
___ Spent $_____ on	___ Spent $_____ on	___ Spent $_____ on	___ Spent $_____ on	___ Spent $_____ on	___ Spent $_____ on	___ Spent $_____ on
___ Spent $_____ on	___ Spent $_____ on	___ Spent $_____ on	___ Spent $_____ on	___ Spent $_____ on	___ Spent $_____ on	___ Spent $_____ on
___ Spent $_____ on	___ Spent $_____ on	___ Spent $_____ on	___ Spent $_____ on	___ Spent $_____ on	___ Spent $_____ on	___ Spent $_____ on

March-Monthly Reflection

Use your calendar to add up the total amount spent this month that was not a part of your budget.

Total Spent _____

Take a look at your monthly spending calendar. What are your thoughts on your monthly spending? How will this influence your choices for next month?

_____
_____
_____
_____
_____
_____
_____
_____

Use your monthly savings tracker to add up the total amount you saved this month.

Total Saved _____

Did you meet your monthly savings goal? What can be done? Go back and look at your monthly budget to make sure you have set a realistic savings goal.

_____
_____
_____
_____
_____
_____
_____

Remember to celebrate success. What thing (within your budget) will you do to reward yourself for taking control of your financial future?

_____
_____
_____

April-Monthly Budget

Item	Company Name	Date	Amount Paid
1. House/Rent			
2. Security Alarm			
3. Utilities			
4. Cable/Internet			
5. Home Phone			
6. Cell Phone			
7. Auto Payment #1			
8. Auto Payment #2			
9. Auto Insurance			
10. Home Warranty/Renters Insurance			
11. Life Insurance			
12. Student Loan #1			
13. Student Loan # 2			
14. Credit Card #1			
15. Credit Card #2			
16. Credit Card #3			
17. Credit Card #4			
18. Credit Card #5			
19. Household/Miscellaneous			
20. Gas			
21. Groceries			
22. Emergency Fund			
23. Savings			
24. Retirement Fund			
25. Entertainment			
26. Other			
27. Other			
28. Other			
29. Other			
30. Other			

Total Monthly Expenses _____

April-Monthly Savings Record Keeping

Designate a savings account specifically for depositing money for your savings goal. This money should not be combined with your emergency fund mentioned on the monthly budget. The goal is to refrain from withdrawing money from this account. However, if it is imperative that you withdraw money, record this as a debit to the account and calculate the new total.

Date	Amount (+, -)	Total

Amount Saved _____

April						
S	M	T	W	T	F	S
___ Spent $_____ on	___ Spent $_____ on	___ Spent $_____ on	___ Spent $_____ on	___ Spent $_____ on	___ Spent $_____ on	___ Spent $_____ on
___ Spent $_____ on	___ Spent $_____ on	___ Spent $_____ on	___ Spent $_____ on	___ Spent $_____ on	___ Spent $_____ on	___ Spent $_____ on
___ Spent $_____ on	___ Spent $_____ on	___ Spent $_____ on	___ Spent $_____ on	___ Spent $_____ on	___ Spent $_____ on	___ Spent $_____ on
___ Spent $_____ on	___ Spent $_____ on	___ Spent $_____ on	___ Spent $_____ on	___ Spent $_____ on	___ Spent $_____ on	___ Spent $_____ on
___ Spent $_____ on	___ Spent $_____ on	___ Spent $_____ on	___ Spent $_____ on	___ Spent $_____ on	___ Spent $_____ on	___ Spent $_____ on
___ Spent $_____ on	___ Spent $_____ on	___ Spent $_____ on	___ Spent $_____ on	___ Spent $_____ on	___ Spent $_____ on	___ Spent $_____ on

April-Monthly Reflection

Use your calendar to add up the total amount spent this month that was not a part of your budget.

Total Spent _____

Take a look at your monthly spending calendar. What are your thoughts on your monthly spending? How will this influence your choices for next month?

_____

_____

_____

_____

_____

_____

_____

Use your monthly savings tracker to add up the total amount you saved this month.

Total Saved _____

Did you meet your monthly savings goal? What can be done? Go back and look at your monthly budget to make sure you have set a realistic savings goal.

_____

_____

_____

_____

_____

_____

_____

Remember to celebrate success. What thing (within your budget) will you do to reward yourself for taking control of your financial future?

_____

_____

_____

May-Monthly Budget

Item	Company Name	Date	Amount Paid
1. House/Rent			
2. Security Alarm			
3. Utilities			
4. Cable/Internet			
5. Home Phone			
6. Cell Phone			
7. Auto Payment #1			
8. Auto Payment #2			
9. Auto Insurance			
10. Home Warranty/Renters Insurance			
11. Life Insurance			
12. Student Loan #1			
13. Student Loan # 2			
14. Credit Card #1			
15. Credit Card #2			
16. Credit Card #3			
17. Credit Card #4			
18. Credit Card #5			
19. Household/Miscellaneous			
20. Gas			
21. Groceries			
22. Emergency Fund			
23. Savings			
24. Retirement Fund			
25. Entertainment			
26. Other			
27. Other			
28. Other			
29. Other			
30. Other			

Total Monthly Expenses _____

May-Monthly Savings Record Keeping

Designate a savings account specifically for depositing money for your savings goal. This money should not be combined with your emergency fund mentioned on the monthly budget. The goal is to refrain from withdrawing money from this account. However, if it is imperative that you withdraw money, record this as a debit to the account and calculate the new total.

Date	Amount (+, -)	Total

Amount Saved _____

May						
S	M	T	W	T	F	S
___ Spent $_____ on	___ Spent $_____ on	___ Spent $_____ on	___ Spent $_____ on	___ Spent $_____ on	___ Spent $_____ on	___ Spent $_____ on
___ Spent $_____ on	___ Spent $_____ on	___ Spent $_____ on	___ Spent $_____ on	___ Spent $_____ on	___ Spent $_____ on	___ Spent $_____ on
___ Spent $_____ on	___ Spent $_____ on	___ Spent $_____ on	___ Spent $_____ on	___ Spent $_____ on	___ Spent $_____ on	___ Spent $_____ on
___ Spent $_____ on	___ Spent $_____ on	___ Spent $_____ on	___ Spent $_____ on	___ Spent $_____ on	___ Spent $_____ on	___ Spent $_____ on
___ Spent $_____ on	___ Spent $_____ on	___ Spent $_____ on	___ Spent $_____ on	___ Spent $_____ on	___ Spent $_____ on	___ Spent $_____ on
___ Spent $_____ on	___ Spent $_____ on	___ Spent $_____ on	___ Spent $_____ on	___ Spent $_____ on	___ Spent $_____ on	___ Spent $_____ on

May-Monthly Reflection

Use your calendar to add up the total amount spent this month that was not a part of your budget.

Total Spent _____

Take a look at your monthly spending calendar. What are your thoughts on your monthly spending? How will this influence your choices for next month?

_____
_____
_____
_____
_____
_____
_____
_____

Use your monthly savings tracker to add up the total amount you saved this month.

Total Saved _____

Did you meet your monthly savings goal? What can be done? Go back and look at your monthly budget to make sure you have set a realistic savings goal.

_____
_____
_____
_____
_____
_____
_____

Remember to celebrate success. What thing (within your budget) will you do to reward yourself for taking control of your financial future?

_____
_____
_____

June-Monthly Budget

Item	Company Name	Date	Amount Paid
1. House/Rent			
2. Security Alarm			
3. Utilities			
4. Cable/Internet			
5. Home Phone			
6. Cell Phone			
7. Auto Payment #1			
8. Auto Payment #2			
9. Auto Insurance			
10. Home Warranty/Renters Insurance			
11. Life Insurance			
12. Student Loan #1			
13. Student Loan # 2			
14. Credit Card #1			
15. Credit Card #2			
16. Credit Card #3			
17. Credit Card #4			
18. Credit Card #5			
19. Household/Miscellaneous			
20. Gas			
21. Groceries			
22. Emergency Fund			
23. Savings			
24. Retirement Fund			
25. Entertainment			
26. Other			
27. Other			
28. Other			
29. Other			
30. Other			

Total Monthly Expenses _____

June-Monthly Savings Record Keeping

Designate a savings account specifically for depositing money for your savings goal. This money should not be combined with your emergency fund mentioned on the monthly budget. The goal is to refrain from withdrawing money from this account. However, if it is imperative that you withdraw money, record this as a debit to the account and calculate the new total.

Date	Amount (+, -)	Total

Amount Saved _____

June						
S	M	T	W	T	F	S
__ Spent $_____ on	__ Spent $_____ on	__ Spent $_____ on	__ Spent $_____ on	__ Spent $_____ on	__ Spent $_____ on	__ Spent $_____ on
__ Spent $_____ on	__ Spent $_____ on	__ Spent $_____ on	__ Spent $_____ on	__ Spent $_____ on	__ Spent $_____ on	__ Spent $_____ on
__ Spent $_____ on	__ Spent $_____ on	__ Spent $_____ on	__ Spent $_____ on	__ Spent $_____ on	__ Spent $_____ on	__ Spent $_____ on
__ Spent $_____ on	__ Spent $_____ on	__ Spent $_____ on	__ Spent $_____ on	__ Spent $_____ on	__ Spent $_____ on	__ Spent $_____ on
__ Spent $_____ on	__ Spent $_____ on	__ Spent $_____ on	__ Spent $_____ on	__ Spent $_____ on	__ Spent $_____ on	__ Spent $_____ on
__ Spent $_____ on	__ Spent $_____ on	__ Spent $_____ on	__ Spent $_____ on	__ Spent $_____ on	__ Spent $_____ on	__ Spent $_____ on

June-Monthly Reflection

Use your calendar to add up the total amount spent this month that was not a part of your budget.

Total Spent _____

Take a look at your monthly spending calendar. What are your thoughts on your monthly spending? How will this influence your choices for next month?

_____
_____
_____
_____
_____
_____
_____

Use your monthly savings tracker to add up the total amount you saved this month.

Total Saved _____

Did you meet your monthly savings goal? What can be done? Go back and look at your monthly budget to make sure you have set a realistic savings goal.

_____
_____
_____
_____
_____
_____
_____

Remember to celebrate success. What thing (within your budget) will you do to reward yourself for taking control of your financial future?

_____
_____
_____

July-Monthly Budget

Item	Company Name	Date	Amount Paid
1. House/Rent			
2. Security Alarm			
3. Utilities			
4. Cable/Internet			
5. Home Phone			
6. Cell Phone			
7. Auto Payment #1			
8. Auto Payment #2			
9. Auto Insurance			
10. Home Warranty/Renters Insurance			
11. Life Insurance			
12. Student Loan #1			
13. Student Loan #2			
14. Credit Card #1			
15. Credit Card #2			
16. Credit Card #3			
17. Credit Card #4			
18. Credit Card #5			
19. Household/Miscellaneous			
20. Gas			
21. Groceries			
22. Emergency Fund			
23. Savings			
24. Retirement Fund			
25. Entertainment			
26. Other			
27. Other			
28. Other			
29. Other			
30. Other			

Total Monthly Expenses _____

July-Monthly Savings Record Keeping

Designate a savings account specifically for depositing money for your savings goal. This money should not be combined with your emergency fund mentioned on the monthly budget. The goal is to refrain from withdrawing money from this account. However, if it is imperative that you withdraw money, record this as a debit to the account and calculate the new total.

Date	Amount (+, -)	Total

Amount Saved _____

July						
S	M	T	W	T	F	S
___ Spent $_____ on	___ Spent $_____ on	___ Spent $_____ on	___ Spent $_____ on	___ Spent $_____ on	___ Spent $_____ on	___ Spent $_____ on
___ Spent $_____ on	___ Spent $_____ on	___ Spent $_____ on	___ Spent $_____ on	___ Spent $_____ on	___ Spent $_____ on	___ Spent $_____ on
___ Spent $_____ on	___ Spent $_____ on	___ Spent $_____ on	___ Spent $_____ on	___ Spent $_____ on	___ Spent $_____ on	___ Spent $_____ on
___ Spent $_____ on	___ Spent $_____ on	___ Spent $_____ on	___ Spent $_____ on	___ Spent $_____ on	___ Spent $_____ on	___ Spent $_____ on
___ Spent $_____ on	___ Spent $_____ on	___ Spent $_____ on	___ Spent $_____ on	___ Spent $_____ on	___ Spent $_____ on	___ Spent $_____ on
___ Spent $_____ on	___ Spent $_____ on	___ Spent $_____ on	___ Spent $_____ on	___ Spent $_____ on	___ Spent $_____ on	___ Spent $_____ on

July-Monthly Reflection

Use your calendar to add up the total amount spent this month that was not a part of your budget.

Total Spent _____

Take a look at your monthly spending calendar. What are your thoughts on your monthly spending? How will this influence your choices for next month?

_____

_____

_____

_____

_____

_____

_____

Use your monthly savings tracker to add up the total amount you saved this month.

Total Saved _____

Did you meet your monthly savings goal? What can be done? Go back and look at your monthly budget to make sure you have set a realistic savings goal.

_____

_____

_____

_____

_____

_____

_____

Remember to celebrate success. What thing (within your budget) will you do to reward yourself for taking control of your financial future?

_____

_____

_____

August-Monthly Budget

Item	Company Name	Date	Amount Paid
1. House/Rent			
2. Security Alarm			
3. Utilities			
4. Cable/Internet			
5. Home Phone			
6. Cell Phone			
7. Auto Payment #1			
8. Auto Payment #2			
9. Auto Insurance			
10. Home Warranty/Renters Insurance			
11. Life Insurance			
12. Student Loan #1			
13. Student Loan # 2			
14. Credit Card #1			
15. Credit Card #2			
16. Credit Card #3			
17. Credit Card #4			
18. Credit Card #5			
19. Household/Miscellaneous			
20. Gas			
21. Groceries			
22. Emergency Fund			
23. Savings			
24. Retirement Fund			
25. Entertainment			
26. Other			
27. Other			
28. Other			
29. Other			
30. Other			

Total Monthly Expenses _____

August-Monthly Savings Record Keeping

Designate a savings account specifically for depositing money for your savings goal. This money should not be combined with your emergency fund mentioned on the monthly budget. The goal is to refrain from withdrawing money from this account. However, if it is imperative that you withdraw money, record this as a debit to the account and calculate the new total.

Date	Amount (+, -)	Total

Amount Saved _____

August						
S	M	T	W	T	F	S
___ Spent $_____ on	___ Spent $_____ on	___ Spent $_____ on	___ Spent $_____ on	___ Spent $_____ on	___ Spent $_____ on	___ Spent $_____ on
___ Spent $_____ on	___ Spent $_____ on	___ Spent $_____ on	___ Spent $_____ on	___ Spent $_____ on	___ Spent $_____ on	___ Spent $_____ on
___ Spent $_____ on	___ Spent $_____ on	___ Spent $_____ on	___ Spent $_____ on	___ Spent $_____ on	___ Spent $_____ on	___ Spent $_____ on
___ Spent $_____ on	___ Spent $_____ on	___ Spent $_____ on	___ Spent $_____ on	___ Spent $_____ on	___ Spent $_____ on	___ Spent $_____ on
___ Spent $_____ on	___ Spent $_____ on	___ Spent $_____ on	___ Spent $_____ on	___ Spent $_____ on	___ Spent $_____ on	___ Spent $_____ on
___ Spent $_____ on	___ Spent $_____ on	___ Spent $_____ on	___ Spent $_____ on	___ Spent $_____ on	___ Spent $_____ on	___ Spent $_____ on

August-Monthly Reflection

Use your calendar to add up the total amount spent this month that was not a part of your budget.

Total Spent _____

Take a look at your monthly spending calendar. What are your thoughts on your monthly spending? How will this influence your choices for next month?

_____
_____
_____
_____
_____
_____
_____
_____

Use your monthly savings tracker to add up the total amount you saved this month.

Total Saved _____

Did you meet your monthly savings goal? What can be done? Go back and look at your monthly budget to make sure you have set a realistic savings goal.

_____
_____
_____
_____
_____
_____
_____
_____

Remember to celebrate success. What thing (within your budget) will you do to reward yourself for taking control of your financial future?

_____
_____
_____

September-Monthly Budget

Item	Company Name	Date	Amount Paid
1. House/Rent			
2. Security Alarm			
3. Utilities			
4. Cable/Internet			
5. Home Phone			
6. Cell Phone			
7. Auto Payment #1			
8. Auto Payment #2			
9. Auto Insurance			
10. Home Warranty/Renters Insurance			
11. Life Insurance			
12. Student Loan #1			
13. Student Loan # 2			
14. Credit Card #1			
15. Credit Card #2			
16. Credit Card #3			
17. Credit Card #4			
18. Credit Card #5			
19. Household/Miscellaneous			
20. Gas			
21. Groceries			
22. Emergency Fund			
23. Savings			
24. Retirement Fund			
25. Entertainment			
26. Other			
27. Other			
28. Other			
29. Other			
30. Other			

Total Monthly Expenses _____

September-Monthly Savings Record Keeping

Designate a savings account specifically for depositing money for your savings goal. This money should not be combined with your emergency fund mentioned on the monthly budget. The goal is to refrain from withdrawing money from this account. However, if it is imperative that you withdraw money, record this as a debit to the account and calculate the new total.

Date	Amount (+, -)	Total

Amount Saved _____

September						
S	M	T	W	T	F	S
___ Spent $_____ on	___ Spent $_____ on	___ Spent $_____ on	___ Spent $_____ on	___ Spent $_____ on	___ Spent $_____ on	___ Spent $_____ on
___ Spent $_____ on	___ Spent $_____ on	___ Spent $_____ on	___ Spent $_____ on	___ Spent $_____ on	___ Spent $_____ on	___ Spent $_____ on
___ Spent $_____ on	___ Spent $_____ on	___ Spent $_____ on	___ Spent $_____ on	___ Spent $_____ on	___ Spent $_____ on	___ Spent $_____ on
___ Spent $_____ on	___ Spent $_____ on	___ Spent $_____ on	___ Spent $_____ on	___ Spent $_____ on	___ Spent $_____ on	___ Spent $_____ on
___ Spent $_____ on	___ Spent $_____ on	___ Spent $_____ on	___ Spent $_____ on	___ Spent $_____ on	___ Spent $_____ on	___ Spent $_____ on
___ Spent $_____ on	___ Spent $_____ on	___ Spent $_____ on	___ Spent $_____ on	___ Spent $_____ on	___ Spent $_____ on	___ Spent $_____ on

September-Monthly Reflection

Use your calendar to add up the total amount spent this month that was not a part of your budget.

Total Spent _____

Take a look at your monthly spending calendar. What are your thoughts on your monthly spending? How will this influence your choices for next month?

_____

_____

_____

_____

_____

_____

_____

Use your monthly savings tracker to add up the total amount you saved this month.

Total Saved _____

Did you meet your monthly savings goal? What can be done? Go back and look at your monthly budget to make sure you have set a realistic savings goal.

_____

_____

_____

_____

_____

_____

Remember to celebrate success. What thing (within your budget) will you do to reward yourself for taking control of your financial future?

_____

_____

_____

October-Monthly Budget

Item	Company Name	Date	Amount Paid
1. House/Rent			
2. Security Alarm			
3. Utilities			
4. Cable/Internet			
5. Home Phone			
6. Cell Phone			
7. Auto Payment #1			
8. Auto Payment #2			
9. Auto Insurance			
10. Home Warranty/Renters Insurance			
11. Life Insurance			
12. Student Loan #1			
13. Student Loan #2			
14. Credit Card #1			
15. Credit Card #2			
16. Credit Card #3			
17. Credit Card #4			
18. Credit Card #5			
19. Household/Miscellaneous			
20. Gas			
21. Groceries			
22. Emergency Fund			
23. Savings			
24. Retirement Fund			
25. Entertainment			
26. Other			
27. Other			
28. Other			
29. Other			
30. Other			

Total Monthly Expenses _____

October-Monthly Savings Record Keeping

Designate a savings account specifically for depositing money for your savings goal. This money should not be combined with your emergency fund mentioned on the monthly budget. The goal is to refrain from withdrawing money from this account. However, if it is imperative that you withdraw money, record this as a debit to the account and calculate the new total.

Date	Amount (+, -)	Total

Amount Saved _____

October						
S	M	T	W	T	F	S
— Spent $____ on	— Spent $____ on	— Spent $____ on	— Spent $____ on	— Spent $____ on	— Spent $____ on	— Spent $____ on
— Spent $____ on	— Spent $____ on	— Spent $____ on	— Spent $____ on	— Spent $____ on	— Spent $____ on	— Spent $____ on
— Spent $____ on	— Spent $____ on	— Spent $____ on	— Spent $____ on	— Spent $____ on	— Spent $____ on	— Spent $____ on
— Spent $____ on	— Spent $____ on	— Spent $____ on	— Spent $____ on	— Spent $____ on	— Spent $____ on	— Spent $____ on
— Spent $____ on	— Spent $____ on	— Spent $____ on	— Spent $____ on	— Spent $____ on	— Spent $____ on	— Spent $____ on
— Spent $____ on	— Spent $____ on	— Spent $____ on	— Spent $____ on	— Spent $____ on	— Spent $____ on	— Spent $____ on

October-Monthly Reflection

Use your calendar to add up the total amount spent this month that was not a part of your budget.

Total Spent _____

Take a look at your monthly spending calendar. What are your thoughts on your monthly spending? How will this influence your choices for next month?

_____

_____

_____

_____

_____

_____

_____

Use your monthly savings tracker to add up the total amount you saved this month.

Total Saved _____

Did you meet your monthly savings goal? What can be done? Go back and look at your monthly budget to make sure you have set a realistic savings goal.

_____

_____

_____

_____

_____

_____

_____

Remember to celebrate success. What thing (within your budget) will you do to reward yourself for taking control of your financial future?

_____

_____

_____

November-Monthly Budget

Item	Company Name	Date	Amount Paid
1. House/Rent			
2. Security Alarm			
3. Utilities			
4. Cable/Internet			
5. Home Phone			
6. Cell Phone			
7. Auto Payment #1			
8. Auto Payment #2			
9. Auto Insurance			
10. Home Warranty/Renters Insurance			
11. Life Insurance			
12. Student Loan #1			
13. Student Loan #2			
14. Credit Card #1			
15. Credit Card #2			
16. Credit Card #3			
17. Credit Card #4			
18. Credit Card #5			
19. Household/Miscellaneous			
20. Gas			
21. Groceries			
22. Emergency Fund			
23. Savings			
24. Retirement Fund			
25. Entertainment			
26. Other			
27. Other			
28. Other			
29. Other			
30. Other			

Total Monthly Expenses _____

November-Monthly Savings Record Keeping

Designate a savings account specifically for depositing money for your savings goal. This money should not be combined with your emergency fund mentioned on the monthly budget. The goal is to refrain from withdrawing money from this account. However, if it is imperative that you withdraw money, record this as a debit to the account and calculate the new total.

Date	Amount (+, -)	Total

Amount Saved _____

November						
S	M	T	W	T	F	S
___ Spent $_____ on	___ Spent $_____ on	___ Spent $_____ on	___ Spent $_____ on	___ Spent $_____ on	___ Spent $_____ on	___ Spent $_____ on
___ Spent $_____ on	___ Spent $_____ on	___ Spent $_____ on	___ Spent $_____ on	___ Spent $_____ on	___ Spent $_____ on	___ Spent $_____ on
___ Spent $_____ on	___ Spent $_____ on	___ Spent $_____ on	___ Spent $_____ on	___ Spent $_____ on	___ Spent $_____ on	___ Spent $_____ on
___ Spent $_____ on	___ Spent $_____ on	___ Spent $_____ on	___ Spent $_____ on	___ Spent $_____ on	___ Spent $_____ on	___ Spent $_____ on
___ Spent $_____ on	___ Spent $_____ on	___ Spent $_____ on	___ Spent $_____ on	___ Spent $_____ on	___ Spent $_____ on	___ Spent $_____ on
___ Spent $_____ on	___ Spent $_____ on	___ Spent $_____ on	___ Spent $_____ on	___ Spent $_____ on	___ Spent $_____ on	___ Spent $_____ on

November-Monthly Reflection

Use your calendar to add up the total amount spent this month that was not a part of your budget.

Total Spent _____

Take a look at your monthly spending calendar. What are your thoughts on your monthly spending? How will this influence your choices for next month?

_____
_____
_____
_____
_____
_____
_____

Use your monthly savings tracker to add up the total amount you saved this month.

Total Saved _____

Did you meet your monthly savings goal? What can be done? Go back and look at your monthly budget to make sure you have set a realistic savings goal.

_____
_____
_____
_____
_____
_____
_____

Remember to celebrate success. What thing (within your budget) will you do to reward yourself for taking control of your financial future?

_____
_____
_____

December-Monthly Budget

Item	Company Name	Date	Amount Paid
1. House/Rent			
2. Security Alarm			
3. Utilities			
4. Cable/Internet			
5. Home Phone			
6. Cell Phone			
7. Auto Payment #1			
8. Auto Payment #2			
9. Auto Insurance			
10. Home Warranty/Renters Insurance			
11. Life Insurance			
12. Student Loan #1			
13. Student Loan # 2			
14. Credit Card #1			
15. Credit Card #2			
16. Credit Card #3			
17. Credit Card #4			
18. Credit Card #5			
19. Household/Miscellaneous			
20. Gas			
21. Groceries			
22. Emergency Fund			
23. Savings			
24. Retirement Fund			
25. Entertainment			
26. Other			
27. Other			
28. Other			
29. Other			
30. Other			

Total Monthly Expenses _____

December-Monthly Savings Record Keeping

Designate a savings account specifically for depositing money for your savings goal. This money should not be combined with your emergency fund mentioned on the monthly budget. The goal is to refrain from withdrawing money from this account. However, if it is imperative that you withdraw money, record this as a debit to the account and calculate the new total.

Date	Amount (+, -)	Total

Amount Saved _____

			December			
S	M	T	W	T	F	S
___ Spent $_____ on	___ Spent $_____ on	___ Spent $_____ on	___ Spent $_____ on	___ Spent $_____ on	___ Spent $_____ on	___ Spent $_____ on
___ Spent $_____ on	___ Spent $_____ on	___ Spent $_____ on	___ Spent $_____ on	___ Spent $_____ on	___ Spent $_____ on	___ Spent $_____ on
___ Spent $_____ on	___ Spent $_____ on	___ Spent $_____ on	___ Spent $_____ on	___ Spent $_____ on	___ Spent $_____ on	___ Spent $_____ on
___ Spent $_____ on	___ Spent $_____ on	___ Spent $_____ on	___ Spent $_____ on	___ Spent $_____ on	___ Spent $_____ on	___ Spent $_____ on
___ Spent $_____ on	___ Spent $_____ on	___ Spent $_____ on	___ Spent $_____ on	___ Spent $_____ on	___ Spent $_____ on	___ Spent $_____ on
___ Spent $_____ on	___ Spent $_____ on	___ Spent $_____ on	___ Spent $_____ on	___ Spent $_____ on	___ Spent $_____ on	___ Spent $_____ on

December-Monthly Reflection

Use your calendar to add up the total amount spent this month that was not a part of your budget.

Total Spent _____

Take a look at your monthly spending calendar. What are your thoughts on your monthly spending? How will this influence your choices for next month?

_____
_____
_____
_____
_____
_____
_____

Use your monthly savings tracker to add up the total amount you saved this month.

Total Saved _____

Did you meet your monthly savings goal? What can be done? Go back and look at your monthly budget to make sure you have set a realistic savings goal.

_____
_____
_____
_____
_____
_____
_____

Remember to celebrate success. What thing (within your budget) will you do to reward yourself for taking control of your financial future?

_____
_____
_____

End of Year Reflection

Take a look back over your financial year. What are your overall thoughts of your financial actions?

_____
_____
_____
_____
_____
_____

Did you meet your savings goal? If not, what factors contributed to this outcome?

_____
_____
_____

Take a look at your monthly budgets. Did you decrease or eliminate any bills? Did you create any new bills? What are your thoughts on your ability to stick to your monthly budget?

_____
_____
_____

How will you use this information to plan for the year ahead?

_____
_____
_____
_____

Notes

Notes

Notes

Notes

Important Numbers

Company Name	Number